Indiana

English/Language Arts

8

TEACHER'S GUIDE

Harcourt Achieve

Rigby • Steck-Vaughn

www.HarcourtAchieve.com
1.800.531.5015

ISBN 0-7398-9647-4

1 2 3 4 5 6 7 8 9 10 355 11 10 09 08 07 06 05

Achieve Indiana
Contents

Program Features

With ACHIEVE Indiana, you can . . .

- help your students succeed on the **Indiana Statewide Testing for Educational Progress-Plus** *(ISTEP+)* English/Language Arts test.

- meet the mandates of the **No Child Left Behind Act (NCLB).**

- monitor your students' **Adequate Yearly Progress (AYP)** in reading proficiency.

Begin with Modeled Instruction . . . That Matches the Indiana Standards!

- items correlated to **Indiana** English/Language Arts Standards

- instructional tips for all items that teach how to arrive at the correct answer

- **Indiana** Standards cited on every page

Have Student Take a Practice Test . . . That Simulates an ISTEP+ Test!

- each item keyed to an **Indiana** Standard

- content and design of the *ISTEP+* English/Language Arts test

Follow Up with Additional Support . . . That Emphasizes the Indiana Standards!

- detailed answer explanations for all items—a further opportunity for instruction

- standards identified for reteaching opportunities

STANDARDS FOR *Indiana English/Language Arts*

Standard 1

Students use their knowledge of word parts and word relationships, as well as context clues, to determine the meaning of specialized vocabulary and to understand the precise meaning of grade-level-appropriate words.

7.1.1 **Vocabulary and Concept Development.** Identify and understand idioms and comparisons—such as analogies, metaphors, and similes—in prose and poetry.

7.1.2 **Vocabulary and Concept Development.** Use knowledge of Greek, Latin, and Anglo-Saxon roots and word parts to understand subject-area vocabulary (science, social studies, and mathematics).

7.1.3 **Vocabulary and Concept Development.** Clarify word meanings through the use of definition, example, restatement, or the use of contrast stated in the text.

Standard 2

Students read and understand grade-level-appropriate material.

7.2.1 **Structural Features of Informational and Technical Materials.** Understand and analyze the differences in structure and purpose between various categories of informational materials (such as textbooks, newspapers, and instructional or technical manuals).

7.2.2 **Structural Features of Informational and Technical Materials.** Locate information by using a variety of consumer and public documents.

7.2.3 **Structural Features of Informational and Technical Materials.** Analyze text that uses the cause-and-effect organizational pattern.

7.2.4 **Comprehension and Analysis of Grade-Level-Appropriate Text.** Identify and trace the development of an author's argument, point of view, or perspective in text.

7.2.5 **Comprehension and Analysis of Grade-Level-Appropriate Text.** Understand and explain the use of a simple mechanical device by following directions in a technical manual.

7.2.6 **Expository (Informational) Critique.** Assess the adequacy, accuracy, and appropriateness of the author's evidence to support claims and assertions, noting instances of bias and stereotyping.

Standard 3

Students read and respond to grade-level-appropriate historically or culturally significant works of literature that reflect and enhance their study of history and social science.

7.3.1 **Structural Features of Literature.** Discuss the purposes and characteristics of different forms of written text, such as the short story, the novel, the novella, and the essay.

7.3.2 **Narrative Analysis of Grade-Level-Appropriate Text.** Identify events that advance the plot and determine how each event explains past or present action or foreshadows (provides clues to) future action.

7.3.3 **Narrative Analysis of Grade-Level-Appropriate Text.** Analyze characterization as shown through a character's thoughts, words, speech patterns, and actions; the narrator's description; and the thoughts, words, and actions of other characters.

7.3.4 **Narrative Analysis of Grade-Level-Appropriate Text.** Identify and analyze themes—such as bravery, loyalty, friendship, and loneliness—which appear in many different works.

7.3.5 **Narrative Analysis of Grade-Level-Appropriate Text.** Contrast points of view—such as first person, third person, limited and omniscient, and subjective and objective—in narrative text and explain how they affect the overall theme of the work.

Standard 4 **Students discuss, list, and graphically organize writing ideas. They write clear, coherent, and focused essays. Students progress through the stages of the writing process and proofread, edit, and revise writing.**

7.4.2 **Organization and Focus.** Create an organizational structure that balances all aspects of the composition and uses effective transitions between sentences to unify important ideas.

7.4.3 **Organization and Focus.** Support all statements and claims with anecdotes (first-person accounts), descriptions, facts and statistics, and specific examples.

7.4.4 **Organization and Focus.** Use strategies of note-taking, outlining, and summarizing to impose structure on composition drafts.

7.4.5 **Research and Technology.** Identify topics; ask and evaluate questions; and develop ideas leading to inquiry, investigation, and research.

7.4.6 **Research and Technology.** Give credit for both quoted and paraphrased information in a bibliography by using a consistent format for citations.

7.4.8 **Evaluation and Revision.** Review, evaluate, and revise writing for meaning and clarity.

7.4.9 **Evaluation and Revision.** Edit and proofread one's own writing, as well as that of others, using an editing checklist or set of rules, with specific examples of corrections of frequent errors.

7.4.10 **Evaluation and Revision.** Revise writing to improve organization and word choice after checking the logic of the ideas and the precision of the vocabulary.

Standard 5

Students write narrative (story), expository (informational), persuasive, and descriptive texts (of at least 500 to 700 words). Writing demonstrates an awareness of the audience and purpose for writing.

7.5.4 **Write persuasive compositions.** State a clear position or perspective in support of a proposition or proposal. Describe the points in support of the proposition, employing well-articulated evidence and effective emotional appeals. Anticipate and address reader concerns and counterarguments.

7.5.6 **Use Writing Strategies.** Use varied word choices to make writing interesting and more precise.

7.5.7 **Use Writing Strategies.** Write for different purposes and to a specific audience or person, adjusting style and tone as necessary.

Standard 6

Students write using Standard English conventions appropriate to the grade level.

7.6.1 **Sentence Structure.** Properly place modifiers (words or phrases that describe, limit, or qualify another word) and use the active voice (sentences in which the subject is doing the action) when wishing to convey a livelier effect.

7.6.2 **Grammar.** Identify and use infinitives (the word *to* followed by the base form of a verb, such as *to understand* or *to learn*) and participles (made by adding *-ing, -d, -ed, -n, -en,* or *-t* to the base form of the verb, such as *dreaming, chosen, built,* and *grown*).

7.6.3 **Grammar.** Make clear references between pronouns and antecedents by placing the pronoun where it shows to what word it refers.

7.6.4 **Grammar.** Identify all parts of speech (verbs, nouns, pronouns, adjectives, adverbs, prepositions, conjunctions, and interjections) and types and structure of sentences.

7.6.5 **Grammar.** Demonstrate appropriate English usage (such as pronoun reference).

7.6.6 **Punctuation.** Identify and correctly use hyphens (-), dashes (—), brackets ([ ]), and semicolons (;).

7.6.7 **Punctuation.** Demonstrate the correct use of quotation marks and the use of commas with subordinate clauses.

7.6.8 **Capitalization.** Use correct capitalization.

7.6.9 **Spelling.** Spell correctly derivatives (words that come from a common base or root word) by applying the spellings of bases and affixes (prefixes and suffixes).

HOW TO USE *the Student Book and Teacher's Guide*

Modeled Instruction for Indiana

Achieve Indiana begins with Modeled Instruction, a section that contains a variety of practice items similar to items found on the *ISTEP+* English/ Language Arts test. In this section, students will practice answering multiple-choice items, short-response items, an extended-response item, and a writing activity. Following each item is a Tip that models for students an effective way to arrive at the correct answer. Also, for your easy reference, a correlation of each item to the Indiana English/Language Arts standards can be found at the bottom of the page.

You can use Modeled Instruction as independent practice and let students work individually through the items and strategies. You can also work through the section as a guided instruction activity in small groups or with the whole class. Discuss each item and how the accompanying Tip focuses the student on what the item is asking and how to arrive at the correct answer.

On pages 13–23 of this guide you will find **Answers and Explanations for Instruction** for each item in Modeled Instruction. The explanations afford an additional opportunity for instruction and are written in language you can use directly with your students. They give details about the correct and incorrect answer choices and can be utilized with individual students, as you guide small groups, or the whole class.

Practice Test for Indiana

Beginning on page 45, *Achieve Indiana* includes a Practice Test that follows the content and design of the *ISTEP+* English/ Language Arts test. The Practice Test consists of 40 multiple-choice items, 4 short-response items, 1 extended-response item, and 1 writing activity. Each multiple-choice item is followed by four options, one of which is correct. Students will answer the items in the multiple-choice component by filling in circles provided in the student book. Students will write their answer to the multiple-choice items, short-response items, extended-response item, and writing activity directly in their student books.

Answers and Explanations for Instruction for all items in the Practice Test are found on pages 24–37 of this guide. Each item is first identified by the Indiana English/Language Arts standard that it tests. Then, explanations are given for the correct and incorrect answer choices. These explanations provide an additional opportunity for individualized instruction.

Rubrics for evaluating the short-response items, extended-response item, and writing activity are included at the end of Answers and Explanations for Instruction on page 38.

ADAPTING ACHIEVE INDIANA INSTRUCTION
for Use with Students with Special Needs

Every student can benefit from reviewing test-taking strategies and taking the *ISTEP+* English/Language Arts practice test. Three types of students, however, require practice tailored to their needs.

Struggling Readers, by definition, are not reading on the grade level at which they will be tested. These students commonly read at least two grade levels below the testing level. When a struggling reader reads aloud, you will undoubtedly observe the student's lack of reading fluency, difficulty sounding out grade-level words, and failure to recognize common sight words. Struggling readers often read so slowly they cannot keep track of a paragraph's or even a sentence's content. This seriously hampers their ability to comprehend what they read. Because some of these readers have no diagnosed learning disabilities, they may not receive accommodations such as more time to test or assisting devices such as dictionaries.

English Language Learners (ELLs) present a unique challenge because their levels of reading proficiency vary greatly. Some are fluent readers in their native languages and transfer these skills readily to English, but still may be puzzled by idioms and figures of speech. Others, like struggling readers, read below grade level and are still trying to master word-level comprehension.

ELLs also face unique challenges in taking tests. First, ELLs may lack the background knowledge necessary for full understanding of a passage if it relies on unfamiliar cultural experiences. Second, vocabulary and concepts common to a specific grade level might not be in place in the second language. Third, literary grammatical structures may not resemble the oral language with which they are familiar. Finally, the testing format is often unfamiliar in the home culture.

Although it is impossible to remove all testing obstacles for these students, most test items are written to avoid idioms and ambiguous language. To the extent possible, test items are written to avoid reliance on prior cultural knowledge.

Students with Specific Learning Disabilities (SLDs) usually have average or above-average intelligence but are often hindered by some level of language difficulty. Students may have trouble with semantics, phonology, syntax, or morphology; these types of difficulties are often interrelated. Students with problems in one area will likely have problems in another area. Students may struggle with input, or receptive language. They may have trouble distinguishing letters, or they may read lines repeatedly or skip lines. Other students receive language smoothly but have trouble organizing it. These students struggle with sequencing and have trouble inferring meaning from texts. Other students have memory deficits in working, short-term, or long-term memory.

Some SLDs cause output problems in spatial orientation and fine motor control, meaning that students may test well but have trouble recording answers correctly in standardized test answer booklets. Many students with SLDs must also overcome a lack of motivation and confidence as a result of years of academic struggle. They frequently rely heavily on teachers for guidance and require a great deal of positive reinforcement.

Because these students have identified disabilities, accommodations can be made for them in testing and in practicing for tests. Students' Individualized Education Plans (IEPs) identify appropriate accommodations, including more time to test, alternate forms of recording answers, and the use of assisting devices such as dictionaries and calculators.

Test-Taking Strategies for Students with Special Needs

The test-taking strategies on pages 11–12 of this guide are appropriate for all students, and some are particularly useful for struggling readers, ELLs, and students with SLDs. For example, underlining key words helps distractible readers target important terms and drawing pictures of abstract concepts can help auditory learners and ELLs make sense of content. Model these procedures for students and provide them ample opportunities to practice using them. However, you may need to go beyond general strategies to help your students with special needs succeed. The following suggestions are appropriate for many students with special needs.

■ Use simple sentences that avoid slang, idioms, and negative phrases as you teach these strategies. Speak slowly and pause at logical points to give students time to process and discuss what they hear. Provide written instructions to reinforce verbal instructions and define any terms that may confuse students. When possible, use graphic organizers.

■ Help students build word webs or word banks that explore and link operational words common to test items. For example, a word web for *contrast* would include words and phrases such as *difference, distinguish, tell apart, unalike,* and *compare.* In math, a word web for *add* would include *altogether, sum, plus,* and *in all.* Tell students that learning these words in groups will help them decide quickly and accurately what a test question is asking. Encourage students to look for and underline these key words in test items. This strategy is particularly helpful for ELLs.

■ Help students make a chart of common words and suffixes that identify test items such as *compare and contrast.* For example, *-er, more,*

and *less* form a group that implies comparison and contrast, as do *-est, most,* and *least.* Students should recognize that test items might not use the actual words *compare* or *contrast.*

■ Give students applied practice of tested skills. For example, show students a picture of a common, easily recognized item such as a house or a dog. Ask students to describe the object. What color is it? How big is it? What details can they list? Then show students a picture of the same object that is a different style or type. Have students compare and contrast the two objects. Have students find as many similarities and differences as possible. You may want to use a Venn diagram to record these ideas.

As students become more proficient, guide them through similar exercises involving things they know well but must recall from memory: two musicians or two movies, for example.

■ Ask students whose test-taking skills have improved to guide other students through several test items. Putting the process into their own words by teaching a peer will reinforce the process and build their confidence. Supervise the students' explanations, encouraging them and augmenting their explanations when needed.

■ Teach students to access their prior knowledge about passages they read, math problems they work, and the testing process in general. Use practice test items to lead students to recognize that the items are like many others they have completed in class or on homework.

■ Since the test format itself may intimidate some students, help them achieve a sense of ownership by using the white space on the test pages to their advantage. Reduce students' anxiety by encouraging them to mark on test items, underlining familiar terms, drawing pictures or diagrams when these are helpful, and showing their work as they eliminate incorrect responses.

■ Help students develop strategies for pacing themselves during the test period. Students with special needs can get stuck on a test item and spend too much time on it. Teach students to use a watch or clock to monitor their time.

Time management includes knowing when to skip an item and move on, returning to the skipped item if time allows. Teach students how to skip items and return to them. Students with output processing SLDs especially worry about leaving answers blank and need explicit practice in matching answers to the correct lines.

■ Teach students to break long test passages into more manageable chunks. Practice with students reading a paragraph or a few sentences and underlining key words and phrases. Have students write notes in the margins of the passage to help them remember where key information can be found.

■ A similar strategy can be used for decoding long words with prefixes and suffixes or compound words.

■ Work with students to discover the meaning of unfamiliar words and idioms from the context of the surrounding sentences.

Additional Strategies for Students with Specific Learning Disabilities

■ Review each student's IEP to learn what accommodations are permitted during testing, or ask the student's counselor to provide a list of accommodations. Use these accommodations during the practice test so the student will not be surprised during the actual test.

■ Teach behaviors that help students return to the test item by interrupting their work on the test item, then returning to the beginning of the item rather than picking up where they left off.

■ To alleviate students' anxiety, ensure that the practice test environment is as close to the actual test environment as possible. If students are allowed to record their answers orally on tape, be sure they do so during the practice test. If they are allowed to use manipulatives or assisting devices, be sure to provide them during the practice test.

■ Teach students to segment complex instructions. For example, if a test item requires an extended response that asks students first to compare and then to draw conclusions, model how to find each instruction and mark it, perhaps as "Step 1" and "Step 2." Guide students as they respond to one step at a time and encourage them to review the question after they have recorded their answer to check that part of their answer matches each step. This strategy can also help struggling readers and ELLs.

■ Model each test-taking process and strategy explicitly and repeatedly. Students with SLDs need guidance, repetition, and positive feedback as they tackle standardized testing situations.

PREPARING STUDENTS FOR *the ISTEP+ Practice Test*

Before giving the Practice Test, take some time to discuss these test-taking tips with students.

General Test-Taking Strategies

Time Use

■ Don't spend too much time on any one item

■ Work rapidly but comfortably

■ Return to unanswered items if time permits

■ Use any time remaining to review answers

■ Use a clock to keep track of time

Error Avoidance

■ Pay careful attention to directions

■ Determine clearly what is being asked

■ Mark answers in the appropriate place

■ Check all answers if time permits

Reasoning

■ Read the entire item or passage and all choices before answering

■ Apply what has been learned

Guessing

■ Answer all items on the test

■ Try to eliminate known incorrect answer choices before guessing

Test-Taking Strategies for Multiple-Choice Items

The *ISTEP+* English/Language Arts test contains 40 items in multiple-choice format. Specific strategies can help students work through the multiple-choice items most effectively and efficiently. Here are some helpful strategies to discuss with students.

1. Read all directions thoroughly before answering any items. Misinterpreting directions can lead to incorrect answers.

2. Look for and underline or highlight key words as you read through the passage and item.

3. If an item seems complicated, draw a diagram or picture to represent the item. This can make abstract or confusing concepts seem easier to understand and manage.

4. If an item seems too difficult to answer, skip it and move on to other items. Later, the item may seem easier to answer. If you skip an item, also skip the space for that item in your book. When you finish the test, go back and answer any items you skipped.

5. Make sure your marks are clear and dark and erase any mistakes as thoroughly as possible.

Test-Taking Strategies for Short-Response Items

The *ISTEP+* English/Language Arts test includes 4 short-response items. These strategies can help students work through the short-response items effectively and efficiently. Discuss these strategies with students.

1. Write neatly and clearly.

2. Identify and mark key words as you read the passage and item.

3. If an item seems difficult, create a diagram or picture to represent the item. This can help make confusing ideas seem easier to understand.

Test-Taking Strategies for Extended-Response Item and Writing Activity

The *ISTEP+* English/Language Arts test includes one extended-response item and one writing activity. These strategies can help students work through the extended response item and writing activity effectively and efficiently. Take some time to discuss them with students.

1. Write legibly and clearly.

2. Use available space to plan your responses before you begin writing. For example, you can create webs, outlines, or diagrams.

Administering the ISTEP+ Practice Test

Be sure that each student has the following materials before testing begins:

■ The student book

■ Pencils (with erasers) for marking answers

The test is administered in four sessions. It will take approximately 3 hours and 13 minutes of class time.

Test	Preparation Time	Testing Time
Test 1	5 minutes	32 minutes
Test 2	5 minutes	31 minutes
Test 3	5 minutes	55 minutes
Test 4	5 minutes	55 minutes

Answers and Explanations for Instruction

MODELED INSTRUCTION

Test 1

Science and Technology for All (pages 4–7)

1. ○ Incorrect. The word part *astro* means "outer space." An astronaut is someone who goes into space. He or she would study stars, not flowers, because stars are found in space.
   ○ Incorrect. *Astro* means "outer space." Since stars, not insects, are found in space, astronauts like Mae Jemison go into space and study them.
   ● **Correct. *Astro* means "outer space." Of all the answer choices, only stars are found in space. An astronaut is a person who goes into space and studies stars.**
   ○ Incorrect. In the passage, the writer says that Mae Jemison became an astronaut and went into space. The word part *astro* means "outer space." An astronaut would study stars, not trees, since stars are found in space.

2. ○ Incorrect. A summary states the main idea and supporting details of a passage. This sentence states only one detail about why Mae Jemison studied hard in school.
   ● **Correct. This sentence explains the main idea, that Mae Jemison loves technology, and summarizes the ideas expressed in the supporting details: how Mae Jemison wants others to have access to technology.**
   ○ Incorrect. This sentence states what Mae Jemison tells students. It is one detail from the passage.
   ○ Incorrect. This sentence is only one detail about what Mae Jemison did before she was an astronaut.

3. ○ Incorrect. Statistics are specific numbers representing amounts. This passage includes neither statistics nor summaries of statistics.
   ○ Incorrect. Although the passage is about technology, it does not describe any specific aspect of technology in detail.
   ○ Incorrect. The writer's opinion that Mae Jemison is an inspiring, hard-working person is shown; however, for the most part, the writer describes what Mae Jemison has accomplished. Also, the author's opinion is not compared with anyone else's.
   ● **Correct. The author describes Mae Jemison's interests and work from her childhood to her adulthood. Each event in the passage is one of the series of events that make up Mae Jemison's professional life.**

4. ○ Incorrect. *Accepting* means "enduring without protest or reaction." Jemison became an astronaut by making great efforts; she did not accept the idea that because there were no black female astronauts, she could not be one.
   ● **Correct. An *inspiring* person makes others want to be or do something. Mae Jemison is inspiring because she has achieved important things through hard work. She makes others want to work hard to reach their own goals.**
   ○ Incorrect. *Kind* means "loving, helpful, and nice." Although Jemison may be kind, the writer describes Jemison's professional achievements, not her personality.
   ○ Incorrect. *Loyal* means "faithful." Although Jemison may have faith, the writer talks about what Jemison has given to society, not her personal attitude.

5. ● **Correct. Magazines often include stories about people. This passage has a beginning, a middle, and an end; it tells the story of Mae Jemison's life.**
   ○ Incorrect. A consumer report evaluates a product. No product is mentioned or evaluated in the passage.
   ○ Incorrect. An advertisement tries to persuade a person to buy something. In the passage, the writer describes Mae Jemison's life. He or she does not try to persuade readers to buy something.
   ○ Incorrect. An instruction manual gives the reader step-by-step directions for doing something. This passage does not explain how to do something.

My Most Prized Possession (pages 8–10)

6. ○ Incorrect. Otis wants the autograph because he admires Jackie Robinson. In the passage he is worried, not happy, about the challenge involved in getting the autograph.
   ○ Incorrect. The security guard yells at Otis; he does not encourage Otis to get the autograph.
   ● **Correct. Otis admires Jackie Robinson for being the first Major League baseball player with the same color skin that Otis has. Otis wants to have the autograph to remind him of seeing Robinson play.**
   ○ Incorrect. Uncle Ellwood stays in his seat while Otis attempts to get the autograph. Uncle Ellwood takes Otis to the game; he does not care whether Otis gets the autograph.

7. ○ Incorrect. Other kinds of writing can also be short and include facts. These characteristics alone do not make the passage a short story.
   ● **Correct. A short story is a piece of prose fiction usually under 10,000 words. It includes a plot, setting, and characters.**

○ Incorrect. Rhymes are most often in poems because poems use lyrical language.
○ Incorrect. Statistics are specific numbers representing real amounts. They are not often found in short stories.

8. ○ Incorrect. The number of characters has nothing to do with the story's narrator or point of view.
   ○ Incorrect. When one character, like Jackie Robinson, tells the story and reveals his or her own thoughts, the story is in first person, not third person.
   ○ Incorrect. A third-person narrator is one omniscient voice that knows the thoughts of every character. It is still one narrator.
   ● **Correct. A third-person narrator would tell the events of the entire story and include the perspective of characters other than himself or herself. Besides knowing Otis's thoughts, the reader would know what Uncle Ellwood, the guard, and Jackie Robinson think.**

9. ● **Correct. A *distraction* is something that "draws attention to a different object." A *diversion* is also something that draws attention away from one object and to another. When Otis makes the phone call, he draws the security guard's attention away from Otis and to the phone.**
   ○ Incorrect. An *addition* is something that is added to something else. Otis is not adding anything; he is drawing attention away from himself.
   ○ Incorrect. *Recreation* is free time that "refreshes the spirit." Otis is not relaxing; he is trying to get Jackie Robinson's autograph.
   ○ Incorrect. A *tradition* is a "cultural custom." Otis is not practicing a tradition; he is creating confusion so he can sneak past the guard.

10. ○ Incorrect. Readers learn about how a person must be determined to reach a goal; they do not learn about being generous.

● **Correct. Being determined is an idea about life presented in this story. Otis is determined throughout the story, and his determination results in his successfully getting Jackie Robinson's autograph.**

○ Incorrect. Otis does not wait patiently to see whether he can get Jackie Robinson's autograph. His actions suggest that sometimes it helps to be determined and take action.

○ Incorrect. Otis does not practice kindness throughout the story. This story is about being determined, not being kind.

(pages 11–13)

11. ○ Incorrect. The root word is spelled *believe*. The *e* should follow the *i*.

○ Incorrect. The root word is spelled *believe*. The *e* should follow the *i*. The word *believe* takes the affix *-able*; it drops the final *e*. The affix *un-* is spelled with only one *n*.

● **Correct. The affixes *un-* and *-able* are spelled correctly. The final *e* has been dropped from the word *believe*.**

○ Incorrect. The affix *un-* is spelled with only one *n*. The word *believe* drops the final ending *e* and takes the affix *-able*, not *-ible*.

12. ○ Incorrect. Only spoken words are enclosed by quotation marks; *Ed said* should not be in quotation marks.

● **Correct. Only the spoken words *let's rest for a while* are in quotation marks.**

○ Incorrect. Spoken words should be enclosed in quotation marks. The sentence should end with quotation marks.

○ Incorrect. All spoken words should be inside quotation marks. *I would walk to the store* needs to be enclosed by quotation marks.

13. ○ Incorrect. The sentence needs a direct object that explains what Kai wanted. The verb *train* is in the present tense, so it cannot be the direct object. As a singular noun, it makes no sense.

○ Incorrect. *Trained* is the past tense of *train*.

○ Incorrect. The verb *trains* is in the present tense, so it cannot be the direct object of the sentence. As a plural noun it makes no sense.

● **Correct. *To train* is the infinitive and can function as a noun. It is the direct object in the sentence and makes sense in the context of the sentence.**

14. ○ Incorrect. *In front of the car* is a prepositional phrase that modifies *ran*. It explains where the deer ran, so it should directly follow the phrase that it modifies. The clause *driving down Gray Lane* modifies *car* and should end the sentence.

○ Incorrect. As the sentence reads now, it seems like the deer drives a car in front of another car. The sentence must say that Kevin was driving the car.

○ Incorrect. Modifiers need to be placed as close as possible to the words or phrases they modify. *In front of the car* is a prepositional phrase that modifies *ran*. It explains where the deer ran, so it should directly follow *a deer ran*.

● **Correct. A modifier is a word or phrase that affects the meaning of another word or phrase. Correctly placed modifiers give a sentence one clear meaning. This sentence explains that Kevin was driving the car. When he was driving, a deer ran in front of the car.**

15. ○ Incorrect. An adverb modifies a verb, an adjective, or another adverb. *Right* modifies a noun.
    ● **Correct. An adjective is a word that describes a noun. *Right* describes or limits the noun *field*.**
    ○ Incorrect. A preposition is a word that connects a noun to another word or word group in a sentence. *Right* describes one noun, *field*; it does not link *field* to other words.
    ○ Incorrect. In this sentence, *right* does not show action or a state of being. Therefore it is not a verb. The verb in this sentence is *hit*.

16. ● **Correct. The first word in the sentence and all of the proper nouns—the name of the brother, the city and country, and the name of the company—are capitalized in this sentence.**
    ○ Incorrect. Names of people, places, and things are capitalized. The name *Min*, both parts of the company name *Min's Inventions*, and the name of the city *Seoul* should be capitalized. Also, *brother* is a common noun, not a proper noun, so it should not be capitalized.
    ○ Incorrect. Names of countries are proper nouns and need to be capitalized. The whole name of the company should also be capitalized.
    ○ Incorrect. Both first and last names of people are proper nouns and need to be capitalized. *Min* should be capitalized. The names of cities and countries need to be capitalized. The first word of a sentence is always capitalized.

Test 2
A Most Unusual Woman (pages 14–17)

1. ○ Incorrect. The passage explains that reporters wanted to interview Coleman because she was the first black aviatrix.
   ○ Incorrect. Bessie Coleman learns about other pilots at college before she becomes an aviatrix.
   ● **Correct. The passage explains that Bessie Coleman received much publicity when she came back from France with her pilot's license. She became famous for being the first black aviatrix.**
   ○ Incorrect. In the passage, Bessie Coleman saves money to become a pilot by working as a manicurist in Chicago.

2. ○ Incorrect. In the passage, the author states that Bessie Coleman read about Harriet Quimby at college. The author is telling about Coleman's life, not what colleges teach.
   ● **Correct. Bessie Coleman first read about Harriet Quimby at college. Later, Coleman read that Quimby died in a crash. Both of these experiences motivated Coleman to follow her dream and become a pilot.**
   ○ Incorrect. The author writes about Bessie Coleman's life; he or she does not discuss the dangers of flying in the 1920s.
   ○ Incorrect. The author mentions Harriet Quimby and another aviatrix to show that Bessie Coleman had role models.

3. ○ Incorrect. Bessie Coleman learned how to fly in France and then returned to the United States. The author does not mention French people living in the United States.
   ○ Incorrect. The author states that during Bessie Coleman's lifetime, American society was prejudiced toward women and African Americans. Bessie helped stop the prejudice by becoming a pilot.

Answers and Explanations for Instruction

● **Correct. In the passage, the author states that during the 1920s, women of any race were discouraged from flying in America.**

○ Incorrect. Bessie was an unusual woman because she was one of the first few women to overcome prejudice and become a pilot.

4. ○ Incorrect. These phrases suggest that Bessie was special and reached significant goals, not that she was undignified.

○ Incorrect. The phrases suggest that Bessie achieved something unique; they do not suggest that becoming an aviatrix was humorous.

○ Incorrect. Both phrases suggest that Bessie influenced others in a unique way, making her an important person, not unneeded.

● **Correct.** *Important* **means "having significant worth or consequence." The words** *unusual* **and** *inspiration* **suggest that Bessie Coleman made a significant, worthy contribution to society.**

5. ○ Incorrect. Being interviewed by reporters does not explain why Bessie Coleman inspired other pilots.

● **Correct. In the passage, the author explains that Bessie Coleman worked hard to become a pilot; she overcame prejudice against women and African Americans to reach her goal.**

○ Incorrect. Raymonde de Laroche and Harriet Quimby were role models for Bessie Coleman. They do not explain why Bessie inspired other pilots.

○ Incorrect. Other pilots were inspired by how Bessie Coleman overcame prejudice to become a pilot, not by how she found a job as a manicurist.

Superhero (pages 18–20)

6. ○ Incorrect. A theme is an idea about life that is outlined in a story. Blake specifically teaches readers about encouraging others, not about being honest.

○ Incorrect. Nicknames are not used, created, or discussed in the story.

● **Correct. Encouraging others is an idea about life that is outlined in this story. By telling a story, Blake encourages Tyler to learn how to swim safely in the ocean so that Tyler can enjoy it.**

○ Incorrect. Blake tells Tyler the story in order to encourage him to enjoy swimming in the ocean.

7. ○ Incorrect. In the beginning of the story, Tyler tells Blake that he enjoys swimming in the pool at the park.

○ Incorrect. Blake swims and talks about swimming. Blake does not build a sand castle in the story.

○ Incorrect. Tyler shivers because he is afraid of the waves, not because he is cold. He does not say in the story that he wishes the water were warmer.

● **Correct. Tyler does not enjoy swimming in the ocean because the waves frighten him. Blake is not afraid of the waves in the ocean; he tells a story about how much fun swimming safely in the ocean can be.**

8. ○ Incorrect. Blake tells Tyler a story to reassure him that it is possible to swim safely and happily in the ocean, not to warn Tyler of danger.

● **Correct. Blake's story explains to Tyler how to enjoy swimming safely in the ocean by staying in places where Tyler can touch the bottom.**

○ Incorrect. Tyler is not bored; he is afraid to swim in the ocean.

○ Incorrect. The purpose of the story is to encourage Tyler to swim safely and happily in the ocean.

9. ● Correct. A simile is a comparison that uses the words *like* or *as*. The boy was *like* a cartoon character.
   ○ Incorrect. A metaphor is an implied comparison that does not use the words *like* or *as*.
   ○ Incorrect. An analogy is a comparison of the similar aspects of two different things, not a statement that two things are like each other. *The boy was like one of those fearless cartoon characters* is a statement of similarity, not a comparison of specific aspects of the boy and a cartoon character.
   ○ Incorrect. An idiom is an expression that cannot be understood simply by knowing the meanings of the words in the expression; it is not a direct comparison.

(pages 21–23)

10. ○ Incorrect. The word *finally* suggests that this sentence is not the first sentence of the paragraph. Also, it is clearly a specific detail of the main idea, not a general topic sentence.
    ○ Incorrect. The sentence explains another chore the writer has to do to take care of the dog; it is a detail sentence, not a topic sentence. The word *also* is a clue that this probably is not the first sentence of the paragraph.
    ● Correct. This sentence summarizes the other three sentences about the work that the author does to take care of the dog.
    ○ Incorrect. Because the first part of the sentence suggests that the reader already knows who *her* is, this statement is probably not the first sentence of the paragraph. The first sentence should introduce *her*, the pet dog.

11. ● Correct. A pronoun takes the place of a noun in a sentence. The noun is *girl*, a singular, feminine noun. The singular, feminine possessive pronoun *her* matches *girl*.
    ○ Incorrect. *His* is a singular, masculine pronoun that makes the reader think that the girl gave away someone else's seat.
    ○ Incorrect. *One* is a singular pronoun that can be used for either a masculine or feminine noun. In this sentence, it is unclear whether the seat given up belonged to the girl or someone else.
    ○ Incorrect. *Their* is a plural pronoun; it does not match the singular, feminine noun in the sentence: *girl*.

12. ○ Incorrect. The conjunctive adverb *moreover* needs a semicolon before it and a comma after it. Without these punctuation marks, the two independent clauses run together and form a run-on sentence, or comma splice.
    ○ Incorrect. The conjunctive adverb *moreover* needs a semicolon before it and a comma after it. Without these punctuation marks, the meanings of *moreover* and the sentence are unclear.
    ○ Incorrect. A semicolon must be placed between two independent clauses when a conjunctive adverb like *moreover* is used. The comma before *moreover* creates a run-on sentence or a comma splice, which is incorrect.
    ● Correct. The semicolon is correctly placed between the two independent clauses, and a comma follows *moreover*, a conjunctive adverb.

13. ○ Incorrect. *She* is a single, feminine pronoun. Because both Sara and Ester take singular, feminine pronouns, *she* could refer to either Sara or Ester.
● **Correct. The pronoun *you* follows *Ester*. Since Sara speaks to Ester, it is clear that *you* refers to Ester.**
○ Incorrect. *Ester* should follow *told* without being in quotation marks. *The movie* should follow *like* and should be placed inside the quotation marks. This way, *you* would refer to *Ester*.
○ Incorrect. Spoken words go inside quotation marks. The pronoun *you* should refer to Ester, so *you* should be in quotation marks. As the sentence reads now, *you* refers to the reader.

14. ● **Correct. Four of the five sentences give details about specific parts of serving that the author likes. Sentence 1 is the topic sentence because it tells the main idea of the paragraph: serving the ball is the author's favorite part of tennis.**
○ Incorrect. The topic sentence tells the main idea of a paragraph, in this case, that the author's favorite part of tennis is serving the ball. Sentence 2 mentions throwing a fuzzy ball, but it does not explain the main idea.
○ Incorrect. Sentence 3 describes a detail about the main idea. It is too specific to be a topic sentence.
○ Incorrect. A topic sentence tells the main idea of a paragraph. Sentence 4 tells a specific detail about the main idea.

15. ○ Incorrect. Instructions are given in sequential order so that a person can follow them step-by-step. The next step is to find the third number of the combination and finish unlocking the lock next, not to re-scramble the lock.
○ Incorrect. The directions say that there are three numbers in the combination. The next step is to find the third number to open the lock.

○ Incorrect. In the paragraph, the second step of opening the lock is to point the arrow on the dial to zero. So the next step is to find the third number of the combination, not to locate zero again.
● **Correct. The directions state that there are three numbers in the combination. So, just as the arrow had to point to the first two numbers, the arrow must point to the third number. This choice would most likely help a person find the third number.**

16. ○ Incorrect. A bibliography entry for a book with a single author must include the year in which the book was published. The year should be listed after the publishing company. Also, the author's last name should be listed first, followed by his first name and middle initial.
○ Incorrect. After the title of the book, the city in which the book was published, the publishing company, and the year in which it was published should be listed.
● **Correct. The author's last name is listed first, followed by her first name and middle initial. After the name, the title of the book, city in which it was published, publishing company, and year in which it was published are listed.**
○ Incorrect. The author's last name should be listed first, followed by his first name. The year in which the book was published should follow the publishing company.

Test 3
(pages 24–30)

Sample answer:
Title: Generous Curt Schilling

I think Curt Schilling of the Boston Red Sox should visit our school. Curt Schilling is a starting pitcher and also does a lot of charity work for people with ALS. He has helped raise almost $2 million dollars for people with ALS. I know this because my dad and I are huge fans of the Red Sox. Many Boston Red Sox players do good things, but I like Curt Schilling best.

Curt Schilling was born in the 1960s in Alaska. Then he and his family moved to Arizona. In 1986, he was drafted by the Boston Red Sox, but he didn't stay with them. He played for four other teams including the Philadelphia Phillies and the Arizona Diamondbacks. In 2001, Schilling played in the World Series with the Diamondbacks. The Diamondbacks won the series and Schilling was named co-MVP with Randy Johnson. At the end of 2003, he was traded back to the Boston Red Sox.

While Curt Schilling was playing for the Philadelphia Phillies, he met someone who had ALS. This inspired him to help the Philadelphia ALS Association. He created "Curt's Pitch for ALS," where people donate money for ALS awareness based on the number of strikes he throws and how many games he wins. Curt Schilling donates money to ALS Associations in Philadelphia, Arizona and Massachusetts.

People who have ALS have trouble walking, speaking and breathing. Their muscles shrink and cramp. ALS is not contagious and can affect anyone. The cause of the disease is not known and there is no cure.

Curt Schilling is an inspiration to others because he gives people who have ALS hope. He also gives the friends and families of people who have ALS hope. The hope he gives is that some day there will be a cure for this disease.

He can teach us how we can help others. The community our school is part of always needs help with things. Curt Schilling is a good role model for coming up with creative ways to raise money for important causes.

We should invite Curt Schilling to speak to our school because he is one person who is helping to make a difference in people's lives. And he's a great pitcher.

Answers will vary. Use the rubrics on pages 39–41 to score students' responses.

Test 4

Guests; Dineh, the People (pages 31–37)

1. ○ Incorrect. The story tells how and why Moss learns to respect traditions. While he does listen to others, he listens to them in order to repair the damage he has done to a traditional belt.

   ● **Correct. Throughout the story, Moss takes steps to fix the wampum belt because making wampum belts is a tradition that preserves the history of Moss's people. The reader learns that respecting traditions is a part of life.**

   ○ Incorrect. It is true that the wampum belt is a piece of art, but Moss wants to repair it because it is a traditional piece of art that preserves history. The story focuses on valuing tradition, not art.

   ○ Incorrect. While the wampum belt is made of natural materials, shells, the belt is appreciated because it is a traditional way to preserve history, not because it comes from nature.

2. ○ Incorrect. At the beginning of the story, Moss breaks the belt by touching it. Carrying the beads to Grandfather's house shows that fixing the belt is important. Grandfather may know how to fix it.

○ Incorrect. Moss reveals that he feels guilty in the first part of the story, before he takes the beads to Grandfather.

● Correct. Moss's carrying the beads to Grandfather's house is an important part of the story because it signifies that Grandfather will be able to fix the belt or suggest another way to reverse the damage.

○ Incorrect. Taking the beads to Grandfather suggests that Grandfather will be able to fix the belt, not that he will be angry with Moss.

3. **Sample answer:**

1) The wampum belt is a valued tradition because it helps preserve the oral history of a Native American society.
2) The Baby Laughing Feast is a valued tradition because it demonstrates that the Dineh believe generosity is an important trait.
3) The ceremony for the Blessingway is a valued tradition because it demonstrates that the Dineh believe that bringing harmony to life is an important goal for every person.

Answers will vary. Use the rubric on page 44 to score students' responses.

4. ○ Incorrect. *Accuracy* means "correctness." The second part of the sentence is about how the stars relate to religion, not how correctly they are drawn.

○ Incorrect. *Significance* means "importance." *History* means "a story of past events." In the sentence, the stars represent important religious ideas, not a story of past events.

● Correct. *Significance* means "importance." Both words mean "having meaning." In the article, the stars have an important religious meaning to the Navajo.

○ Incorrect. *Dependence* means "a state of relying on someone or something." The stars have religious importance; they are not dependent on anyone or anything.

5. **Sample answer:**

Why Moss feels bad	Why Grandfather is disappointed
he has disobeyed his parents	he cannot fix the belt
started the day wrong	cannot remember the story it represented
ruined the belt	did not notice the belt enough when it was whole

Answers will vary. Use the rubric on page 44 to score students' responses.

6. ○ Incorrect. Drought is mentioned only as a possible reason why the Anasazi originally abandoned the cliff houses.

○ Incorrect. Although it is clear that the Navajo value hogans for practical and spiritual reasons, this reason alone does not explain why the Navajo would not use empty, perfectly good homes.

● Correct. The author states in the passage that the Navajo fear ghosts and explains that the Navajo burn hogans in which someone has died. The Navajo most likely avoided the cliff houses because they feared the ghosts of the people who had lived and died there.

○ Incorrect. The cliff houses were in the same region in which the Navajo lived, so location is most likely not what the Navajo disliked about the houses.

7. ○ Incorrect. The process through which hogans are built is based on an origin myth. The author explains that it has become a tradition based on literal meaning, not on a spiritual belief.

● **Correct. Searching for hozho, or the Beauty Way, is the best evidence that the Navajo are spiritual because hozho is a spiritual state of being related to religious ideas. The author states that searching for hozho is the Navajo's spiritual life.**

○ Incorrect. It is not clear from the passage why the Navajo chose not to live in the abandoned cliff homes; the author suggests two possible reasons. Because one reason is not stated firmly, the fact that they chose not to live in the cliff homes cannot be used as solid evidence of Navajo spirituality.

○ Incorrect. Using the word "Dineh" is not evidence of spirituality. The author informs the reader that the Navajo call themselves "Dineh" in order to show that the Navajo's unique culture existed before the Spanish met them.

8. ○ Incorrect. Native Americans do not all live in the same kinds of houses. Since the reader is not told which Native American society Moss and his family are part of, the reader cannot assume that Moss lives in a hogan as the Navajo did.

○ The Anasazi are discussed only in the nonfiction article "Dineh, the People." Learning about the Anasazi will not help the reader understand "Guests."

○ Wampum beads are not mentioned in "Dineh, the People," so the article cannot help readers understand the wampum beads in "Guests."

● **Correct. Traditions and rituals are an important part of everyday life in Native American societies. In "Dineh, the People," readers learn about traditions and rituals valued by the Navajo. This helps readers understand why Moss and his family are so serious about fixing the belt, a traditional object.**

Stopping by Woods on a Snowy Evening (pages 38–43)

9. ○ Incorrect. This line from the poem is a statement the speaker makes after explaining that the owner of the woods lives in town. It does not reveal a desire.

○ Incorrect. In this line, the speaker describes why the horse shakes the harness bells; it does not reveal a conflict within the speaker.

○ Incorrect. This line describes what the speaker hears and sees during the snowfall, not how the speaker feels about the snowfall.

● **Correct. The word *but* signals a conflict for the speaker. It follows the speaker's statement that the woods are beautiful and comes just before the speaker reveals that he has promises to keep. The speaker's desire is to stay and watch the woods, but whatever errand the speaker is on must be finished.**

10. **Sample answer:** A theme in the poem is that nature is beautiful and should be appreciated. The speaker enjoys the lovely woods in solitude and does not want to leave them. But duty calls, and the speaker cannot remain.

Answers will vary. Use the rubric on page 44 to score students' responses.

11. ○ Incorrect. These are the first lines of the poem. They describe the setting; they do not discuss the horse at all.
● **Correct. The speaker reveals the horse in the second stanza and suggests to readers that the horse has thoughts about stopping at the woods. This information explains why the horse may shake the bells in the third stanza.**
○ Incorrect. These lines begin the fourth stanza. They explain why the speaker starts going again; they do not mention the horse.
○ Incorrect. These lines are not about the horse. They describe the setting of the poem.

12. **Sample answer:**
1) In stanza two, the speaker explains that it is night, stating that it is "the darkest evening of the year."
2) The speaker describes how quiet and peaceful it is when the only sounds besides the horse's bells are wind and snow. This suggests that the woods are isolated.

Answers will vary. Use the rubric on page 44 to score students' responses.

13. **Sample answer:**
Each stanza of this poem is important because each tells more information about the setting, what the speaker is doing, and how the speaker feels.
First, the speaker explains that snow is falling and he or she is at a woods that someone else owns. However, the owner lives in town so won't see the speaker stop at the woods. Because the owner will not see, the speaker is not worried about stopping on someone else's land.

In the second stanza, the speaker suggests to readers that the horse thinks it odd to stop far away from civilization on this cold night. The speaker uses the horse as a tool to tell readers that other people might judge him or her for staring at trees for no obvious reason. Also, the speaker describes more of the setting in this stanza by mentioning a nearby lake, and the time of the year.

In the third stanza the speaker explains that even though one horse and other people probably think it strange to stop, he or she wants to feel the quiet beauty of the snowfall, adding that there are only two sounds: the bells and the wind.

Finally, the fourth stanza shows readers that the speaker enjoys nature and solitude but is bound to the world by "promises" and "miles" to travel. The repeated last lines make it clear to readers that the speaker would rather watch nature than keep the promises made.

Answers will vary. Use the rubric on pages 41–43 to score students' responses.

PRACTICE TEST

Each item on the Practice Test is correlated to an Indiana English/Language Arts Standard, which appears in boldface type before each answer and explanation.

Test 1
Keep Your Bones Healthy for Life (pages 48–51)

1. **Standard 7.2.3 Analyze text that uses the cause-and-effect organizational pattern.**

   ○ Incorrect. The article explains that getting enough calcium causes bone mass to increase. When bone mass increases, so does density.

   ○ Incorrect. Getting enough calcium causes a teenager to build bone mass. It does not cause a teenager to need more exercise. Both exercising and eating foods that contain calcium build bone mass.

   ● **Correct. The passage explains that increased bone mass is an effect of getting enough calcium.**

   ○ Incorrect. People of all ages need to continue eating foods that contain calcium to maintain healthy bones.

2. **Standard 7.2.6 Assess the adequacy, accuracy, and appropriateness of the author's evidence to support claims and assertions, noting instances of bias and stereotyping.**

   ○ Incorrect. The sentence states that bones are made mostly of calcium, but this alone does not explain why teenagers need to get enough calcium.

   ● **Correct. This sentence explains that bone mass is added during the teenage years. It supports the writer's claim that teenagers need to get enough calcium in order to build strong bones for life.**

   ○ Incorrect. This sentence explains what happens to bones during the adult years. It does not prove that teenagers need to get enough calcium.

   ○ Incorrect. The sentence states that teenagers do not think about their bones. This statement is a generalization, not appropriate evidence for explaining why teenagers need calcium.

3. **Standard 7.2.4 Identify and trace the development of an author's argument, point of view, or perspective in text.**

   ● **Correct. The author wrote the article to explain why and how people should keep their bones healthy. Explaining how calcium affects bones shows readers why getting enough calcium is important.**

   ○ Incorrect. While some of this information may help a student in science class, most of the article explains why and how people should get enough calcium in their diets.

   ○ Incorrect. The author's outlook on aging is positive. He or she is preparing readers to have strong bones in old age, not scaring them about it.

   ○ Incorrect. This action is the opposite of what the author tells readers to do.

4. **Standard 7.1.2 Use knowledge of Greek, Latin, and Anglo-Saxon roots and word parts to understand subject-area vocabulary (science, social studies, and mathematics).**

   ○ Incorrect. *Milli* comes from the Latin word for *thousand*, and it refers to an amount, not a rule.

   ○ Incorrect. *Milli* means "thousandth." It does not refer to an action. It refers to an amount.

Answers and Explanations for Instruction

○ Incorrect. *Milli* means "thousandth." It refers to a mathematical amount, not a location.

● Correct. *Milli* means "thousandth" and comes from the Latin word for "thousand."

The Vision Quest of Swift Feet (pages 53–56)

5. **Standard 7.3.2 Identify events that advance the plot and determine how each event explains past or present action or foreshadows (provides clues to) future action.**

○ Incorrect. Swift Feet walks courageously through the storm because he trusts his guardian spirit to lead him.

○ Incorrect. The hawk leads Swift Feet straight to fire, which he takes home for the benefit of all his people. The walk through the woods is a gift, not trickery.

○ Incorrect. Swift Feet was first visited by his guardian spirit in a dream. He does not discover that the hawk is his guardian spirit during the storm.

● Correct. Swift Feet's guardian spirit helps lead Swift Feet safely through the woods to the sticks on fire. The hawk helps Swift Feet by allowing him to bring fire to his people.

6. **Standard 7.3.3 Analyze characterization as shown through a character's thoughts, words, speech patterns, and actions; the narrator's description; and the thoughts, words, and actions of other characters.**

○ Incorrect. Swift Feet is afraid of the storm and the wild movement of the trees; however, he does not want to run home. He trusts his guardian spirit and walks through the stormy woods.

○ Incorrect. Swift Feet remembers stories about how dangerous storms are, but he cannot find shelter nearby.

● Correct. Although Swift Feet is afraid of the storm's power, he bravely decides to trust his guardian spirit and walk through the storm.

○ Incorrect. Swift Feet is afraid, not cheerful, during the storm. He remembers his elders' stories about how dangerous storms are, but he does not say that he trusts his elders.

7. **Standard 7.3.5 Contrast points of view— such as first person, third person, limited and omniscient, and subjective and objective—in narrative text and explain how they affect the overall theme of the work.**

● Correct. In first-person point of view, the narrator tells the whole story from his or her perspective. Since this is Swift Feet's story, he would tell readers the story, including his thoughts and perspective on the events in the story.

○ Incorrect. In first-person point of view, the narrator or narrators tell the story from the *I* perspective; most short stories have only one narrator.

○ Incorrect. In first-person point of view, only Swift Feet's thoughts would be known because as the main character, he would be telling readers the story and would not know other characters' thoughts.

○ Incorrect. Currently, the story is told by an all-knowing narrator.

8. **Standard 7.1.1 Identify and understand idioms and comparisons—such as analogies, metaphors, and similes—in prose and poetry.**

   ○ Incorrect. An analogy is a comparison of the similar aspects of two different things, not a statement that two things are the same.

   ● **Correct. A metaphor is an implied comparison that does not use the words *like* or *as*. Swift Feet uses a metaphor when he compares the path to a bridge.**

   ○ Incorrect. An idiom is an expression that cannot be understood simply by knowing the meanings of the words in the expression; it is not always used to make comparisons.

   ○ Incorrect. A simile is a comparison that uses the words *like* or *as*.

9. **Standard 7.3.4 Identify and analyze themes—such as bravery, loyalty, friendship, and loneliness—which appear in many different works.**

   ● **Correct. Having courage is an idea about life expressed in this story. Swift Feet shows courage throughout the story, and his courage results in the important ending: bringing fire to his people.**

   ○ Incorrect. Swift Feet is visited by a guardian spirit who helps him find two sticks on fire. Readers do not learn about finding peace; they learn how Swift Feet has the courage to find the fire.

   ○ Incorrect. Swift Feet remembers stories that his elders tell about storms, but he himself does not tell stories.

   ○ Incorrect. Swift Feet is often worried and afraid in the story. He does not teach readers about showing happiness.

(pages 57–59)

10. **Standard 7.6.2 Identify and use infinitives and participles.**

    ○ Incorrect. This sentence needs a direct object, or noun, not another verb. *Wrote* is the past tense of *write* and does not correctly complete the sentence.

    ○ Incorrect. In this sentence, *written* will not fit because it is a participle.

    ● **Correct. In this sentence, the infinitive *to write* functions as the direct object, which is a noun. *To write* is a decision that Pilar made. Pilar decided to write.**

    ○ Incorrect. *Writing* is the present participle of *write*. Although it can function as a gerund—a verb form that can be a noun—it makes no sense in this sentence.

11. **Standard 7.6.1 Properly place modifiers (words or phrases that describe, limit, or qualify another word) and use the active voice (sentences in which the subject is doing the action) when wishing to convey a livelier effect.**

    ● **Correct. A modifier is a word or phrase that affects the meaning of another word or phrase. Correctly placed modifiers give a sentence one clear meaning. In the sentence, Patrick bought apples at the market. He put these apples on the counter.**

    ○ Incorrect. *Which he bought at the market* modifies *apples*, not *counter* and should follow *apples*. As is, the sentence states that Patrick bought the counter, not the apples, at the market.

    ○ Incorrect. This construction implies that Patrick bought the counter at the market.

    ○ Incorrect. As is, the sentence states that the market, not the apples, is on the counter.

12. **Standard 7.6.3 Make clear references between pronouns and antecedents by placing the pronoun where it shows to what word it refers.**

○ Incorrect. *Him* is a single, masculine pronoun, but it is an object pronoun, not a subject pronoun.

○ Incorrect. *He* could refer to someone else other than the teacher and the boy. The second part of the sentence contains unclear pronoun referents *he* and *him*.

● **Correct. The pronoun *you* follows *boy*. Since the first part of the sentence explains that the teacher is saying something to the boy, it is clear that *you* refers to the boy.**

○ Incorrect. *He* is a single, masculine pronoun. Because both of these nouns take singular pronouns, *he* could refer to either the teacher or the boy.

13. **Standard 7.6.5 Demonstrate appropriate English usage (such as pronoun reference).**

○ Incorrect. *Everyone* means "every person," and takes a singular pronoun. *Their* is a plural pronoun and does not match *everyone*.

○ Incorrect. The sentence needs a pronoun. *There* is a word that tells a location; it is not a pronoun.

○ Incorrect. The word *hers* is the possessive form of *she*; it is used when not followed by a noun. In the sentence, the noun *suitcase* follows *hers*. Because of this noun, the correct pronoun to use is *her*.

● **Correct. *Everyone* needs a singular pronoun because it means "every person" and takes a singular verb. In instances when it is unknown whether only males or only females are included, *everyone* needs both a singular masculine and a singular feminine pronoun.**

14. **Standard 7.6.7 Demonstrate the correct use of quotation marks and the use of commas with subordinate clauses.**

● **Correct. A comma precedes the quotation, which is correctly enclosed in quotation marks. Another comma follows the dependent clause, beginning with *because*, separating it from the independent clause, beginning with *he*.**

○ Incorrect. All spoken words should be enclosed in quotation marks. A comma should come after the dependent clause *although it's raining*.

○ Incorrect. The dependent clause starts with *because* and correctly follows the independent clause with no comma; however, the quotation marks should follow the comma after *sick*.

○ Incorrect. Spoken words need to be enclosed in quotation marks. Quotation marks should follow the period after *read*.

15. **Standard 7.2.5 Understand and explain the use of a simple mechanical device by following directions in a technical manual.**

○ Incorrect. Instructions are given in sequential order so that a person can follow them step-by-step. A person would finish setting the time of the clock before adjusting alarm settings.

● **Correct. The directions state that after choosing each number for the time, the "Select" button must be pressed. So, just as the "Select" button needs to be pressed after choosing the hour, the "Select" button would need to be pressed after choosing the minutes.**

○ Incorrect. The first step is checking the clock's batteries to see whether they need to be replaced.

○ Incorrect. A person would finish setting the time before adjusting alarm settings.

16. Standard 7.4.6 Give credit for both quoted and paraphrased information in a bibliography by using a consistent format for citations.

○ Incorrect. A bibliography entry for a book with a single author must include the author's first and last name and the city in which the book was published.

● **Correct. The author's last name is listed first, followed by her first name. After the name, the title of the book, city in which it was published, publishing company, and year in which it was published are listed.**

○ Incorrect. The city in which the book was published must follow the title of the book.

○ Incorrect. An initial in an author's name is listed after the last and first names of the author. Also, the name of the publishing company should follow the city in which the book was published.

Test 2
Swimming with Eels (pages 61–63)

1. **Standard 7.2.6 Assess the adequacy, accuracy, and appropriateness of the author's evidence to support claims and assertions, noting instances of bias and stereotyping.**

○ Incorrect. An anecdote is a short story or piece of information that often comes from a person's life. This sentence is not an anecdote.

○ Incorrect. A stereotype is a general opinion, prejudice, or judgment. The sentence states a specific opinion about a one-of-a-kind exhibit; it is not a stereotypical generalization.

● **Correct. The sentence reveals the writer's opinion that this exhibit is the most exciting exhibit a person can see. The reader or listener is not told why or how this claim is true. Only the writer's opinion supports the claim.**

○ Incorrect. The sentence is an opinion, it does not state a fact that could be proved.

2. **Standard 7.1.3 Clarify word meanings through the use of definition, example, restatement, or through the use of contrast stated in the text.**

○ Incorrect. The word *curious* can mean having "an active desire to learn or to know." The sentences suggest that the animals are special, exciting, and fun to watch. They do not suggest that the eels want to know things.

○ Incorrect. *Athletic* means "vigorous" and "active." The sentence uses the word *glide*, which suggests that the eels swim smoothly, not vigorously or actively, through the water.

● **Correct. The word *sublime* describes something that awes people because of its incredible beauty. A tingling spine is a description that writers sometimes use to show feelings of awe; also, the word *glide* suggests smooth elegance, or beautiful movements.**

○ Incorrect. *Plentiful* means "plenty of" or "abundant." The sentence already states that there are many eels in the exhibit.

3. **Standard 7.2.1 Understand and analyze the differences in structure and purpose between various categories of informational materials (such as textbooks, newspapers, and instructional or technical manuals).**

   ○ Incorrect. A story has characters and a plot. This passage presents information about an exhibit.

   ○ Incorrect. Statistics are specific numbers representing amounts. This passage does not include statistics.

   ○ Incorrect. Only the writer's opinions are given in this passage. The writer indicates that this exhibit is great and that everyone should see it. The writer's opinion is not compared to anyone else's.

   ● **Correct. The passage has short sentences with vivid words. The word *you* makes people believe that they, personally, are invited to see the exhibit. Information in the passage is presented to persuade the audience to visit the exhibit.**

4. **Standard 7.2.2 Locate information by using a variety of consumer and public documents.**

   ○ Incorrect. An encyclopedia article provides readers with facts about a topic.

   ● **Correct. A newspaper includes advertisements. This passage advertises the aquarium exhibit by informing readers about the exhibit and trying to persuade them to visit the exhibit.**

   ○ Incorrect. A children's book tells a story or gives information in language easily understood by children.

   ○ Incorrect. An atlas is a book of maps. This passage does not include a map.

The Party Helper (pages 65–67)

5. **Standard 7.2.4 Identify and trace the development of an author's argument, point of view, or perspective in text.**

   ○ Incorrect. The author's purpose for writing the article is to show others how to start their own businesses. She mentions her business as an example, not an advertisement.

   ● **Correct. The author explains a step in the process of starting a business, and then she uses information about what she did in her own business to explain that step.**

   ○ Incorrect. This article is a how-to guide; it does not ask for readers' opinions or ideas.

   ○ Incorrect. The author uses her business as an example to show readers the kind of problems they may have when they start their own business. In fact, the author makes it clear that she has not always had success.

6. **Standard 7.1.3 Clarify word meanings through the use of definition, example, restatement, or through the use of contrast stated in the text.**

   ○ Incorrect. Dependability is a characteristic of someone on whom another person can rely.

   ○ Incorrect. The word *cheerful* means "full of good spirits." While being happy and optimistic may help a person through the hard parts of starting a business, the author is stating that a person must persevere to reach success.

● Correct. *Persevere* means "to persist," or to "keep trying." A person who has determination is a person who keeps trying to reach a goal. The author tells readers to have determination, to persevere through hard times.

○ Incorrect. If a person demonstrates honesty, then he or she speaks and acts truthfully.

7. **Standard 7.3.1 Discuss the purposes and characteristics of different forms of written text, such as the short story, the novel, the novella, and the essay.**

○ Incorrect. A poem is a text usually written in verses, or stanzas. It uses lyric, descriptive language. This passage uses clear language to explain how-to steps.

● Correct. An essay is a short piece of writing on one subject. It is usually nonfiction. This passage is relatively short and about one topic: starting a business. It is a nonfiction piece because the author is giving her account of starting a business.

○ Incorrect. A novel is a longer prose narrative. It is fiction.

○ Incorrect. A play is performed on a stage by actors. It tells a story through characters' dialogue and plot.

8. **Standard 7.4.4 Use strategies of note-taking, outlining, and summarizing to impose structure on composition drafts.**

○ Incorrect. A summary tells the main idea of a passage and its supporting details. This sentence mentions an idea that is not in the passage.

○ Incorrect. This sentence is the opposite of what the writer says in the passage.

○ Incorrect. The author writes that thinking of a product or service to sell is the first step. A summary tells a main idea, not just one step.

● Correct. This sentence explains that the passage's main idea is how to start a business. It also states that the supporting details are about research, planning, and hard work.

(pages 68–70)

9. **Standard 7.6.7 Demonstrate the correct use of quotation marks and the use of commas with subordinate clauses.**

● Correct. The quotations are enclosed in quotation marks. The first part of the sentence is a dependent clause, and it is correctly followed by a comma, which separates it from both the unspoken words and the independent clause.

○ Incorrect. The name *Frida* should be in the first clause of the sentence so that readers know to whom *she* refers. Quotation marks should be placed before and after quotations.

○ Incorrect. The dependent clause breaks the independent clause into two parts, making the sentence confusing to read. Also, the dependent clause is a quotation and should go inside quotation marks.

○ Incorrect. All quotations need to be enclosed in quotation marks. The word *because* should begin the sentence and turn the first phrase into a dependent clause. Putting *because* at the beginning would explain that living in a suburb, far from downtown, made it necessary for Frida to take the bus.

10. **Standard 7.6.1 Properly place modifiers (words or phrases that describe, limit, or qualify another word) and use the active voice (sentences in which the subject is doing the action) when wishing to convey a livelier effect.**

   ○ Incorrect. Modifiers need to be placed as close as possible to the words they modify. In the sentence, *upholstered in blue leather* modifies *a used car,* so it should follow *a used car.* As it reads now, it seems as though the son is upholstered in blue leather.

   ○ Incorrect. The modifier *upholstered in leather* modifies *a used car,* so it should follow *a used car.* Also, *a used car* should follow *he bought.* As it reads now, the sentence says the son is upholstered in blue leather.

   ○ Incorrect. Modifiers need to be placed as close as possible to the words they modify. *Upholstered in blue leather* modifies *a used car,* so should follow *a used car.* As is, the sentence says that the man was upholstered in blue leather when he bought the car.

   ● **Correct. A modifier is a word or phrase that affects the meaning of another word or phrase. Correctly placed modifiers give a sentence a clear meaning. In the sentence, the man bought his son a used car. The used car was upholstered in blue leather.**

11. **Standard 7.6.9 Spell correctly derivatives (words that come from a common base or root word) by applying the spellings of bases and affixes (prefixes and suffixes).**

   ○ Incorrect. The word *predict* takes the *affix -able,* not *-ible.*

   ● **Correct. The affixes *un-* and *-able,* are added to the root word *predict* without changing their spellings. The root word's spelling does not change.**

   ○ Incorrect. The affix *un-* is spelled with only one *n.* The root word *predict* does not drop the *t* when *-able* is added.

   ○ Incorrect. The affix is spelled *-able,* not *-abel.*

12. **Standard 7.6.6 Identify and correctly use hyphens (-), dashes (—), brackets ([ ]), and semicolons (;).**

   ● **Correct. The semicolon is correctly placed between the two independent clauses, and a comma follows *however,* which is a conjunctive adverb.**

   ○ Incorrect. A comma follows conjunctive adverbs like *however.*

   ○ Incorrect. A semicolon must be placed between two independent clauses when a conjunctive adverb like *however* is used. The comma before *however* creates a run-on sentence or a comma splice, which is incorrect.

   ○ Incorrect. The conjunctive adverb *however* needs a semicolon before it and a comma after it. Without these punctuation marks, the two independent clauses run together and form a run-on sentence or comma splice.

13. **Standard 7.6.8 Use correct capitalization.**

   ○ Incorrect. Proper nouns—names of people, places, and things—are capitalized. The names *Juanita* and *Monet* should be capitalized as well as the name of the museum, *Museum of Fine Art.* Also, the first word of a sentence is always capitalized even when it is not a name.

   ○ Incorrect. First and last names of people are proper nouns and need to be capitalized. *Juanita* should be capitalized. *Paintings* is not a proper noun in this case; it is a common noun. The whole name of the museum should be capitalized.

● **Correct. All proper nouns and the first word are capitalized in this sentence.**

○ Incorrect. Both first and last names of people are proper nouns and need to be capitalized. *Monet* should be capitalized. The entire name of a place needs to be capitalized, so *museum* should be capitalized. In this sentence, *paintings* is a common noun.

14. **Standard 7.4.10 Revise writing to improve organization and word choice after checking the logic of the ideas and the precision of the vocabulary.**

● **Correct. The first sentence of a paragraph is often a general sentence. This sentence summarizes the other three sentences about growing tomato plants.**

○ Incorrect. The word *then* suggests that this sentence is not the first sentence of the paragraph.

○ Incorrect. The sentence is a detail that explains what happens after the tomatoes are planted and before they are eaten.

○ Incorrect. The first part of the sentence suggests that the reader already knows which tomatoes are being discussed, a good sign that this is not the first sentence. It explains what happens after the tomatoes are planted.

15. **Standard 7.6.4 Identify all parts of speech (verbs, nouns, pronouns, adjectives, adverbs, prepositions, conjunctions, and interjections) and types and structure of sentences.**

○ Incorrect. A pronoun takes the place of a noun in a sentence. *For* does not stand for a subject, or noun, in the sentence.

○ Incorrect. An adverb describes a verb, an adjective, or an adverb. *For* does not describe a verb, an adjective, or an adverb.

● **Correct. A preposition is a word that combines with a noun or noun phrase to form a prepositional phrase and explains something important about the sentence. *For* combines with *a bike ride* and explains where Logan decided to go.**

○ Incorrect. A conjunction is a word that joins two or more equal items.

16. **Standard 7.4.8 Review, evaluate, and revise writing for meaning and clarity.**

● **Correct. Three of the four sentences give details about how the writer likes his or her turkey and cheese sandwich. Sentence 1 is the topic sentence because it gives the main idea of the paragraph: what kind of sandwich the author likes to eat.**

○ Incorrect. Sentence 2 describes a detail about the main idea. It is too specific to be a topic sentence.

○ Incorrect. A topic sentence tells the main idea of a paragraph. Sentence 3 tells one specific detail about the main idea.

○ Incorrect. This sentence, too, is one detail about the sandwich.

Answers and Explanations for Instruction

Test 3

Pages (73–79)

Standards 7.4 Writing: Writing Process;
7.5 Writing: Writing Applications; 7.6 Writing:
Written English Language Conventions

Sample answer:

Title: Learning about Our Irish
Ancestors

I would choose for my family to visit Ireland. Ireland is an island in the Atlantic Ocean off the coast of Great Britain. It is not very large, but many people live there, and many people in other countries have ancestors from Ireland.

In fact, my family has ancestors from Ireland—the Ryans. We should visit Ireland because then we could see where our relatives came from before coming to America during the Potato Famine. Besides learning about why our ancestors came to America, my family could also learn about why we practice the religion we do and eat the foods we eat. For example, people from Ireland are often Catholics and like to eat meat and potatoes.

We would see many interesting things in Ireland. We would see memorials to people who died in the Potato Famine. We would see memorials to the immigrants, like my ancestors, who went to other countries during the Potato Famine.

We would see fun things too, like Blarney Castle. Ireland has lots of castles, but Blarney Castle is famous because of the Blarney Stone. The Blarney Stone is at the top of the castle, and a person who kisses the stone is given the gift of gab. (Gabbing means talking). Suddenly, so the story about the Blarney Stone goes, the person can talk circles around other people and tell great stories.

My family and I would also get to see every day life in Ireland today. We would find out what kind of magazines Irish people read and what kind of candy they eat. The houses would look slightly different from American houses because they are built for different weather and a different climate than ours.

Ireland is an interesting and beautiful country. It would be an informative and pleasant trip.

Answers will vary. Use the rubrics on pages 39–41 to score students' responses.

Test 4

A Glimpse of War; Life at Home During the Civil War (pages 81–86)

1. **Standard 7.3.4 Identify and analyze themes—such as bravery, loyalty, friendship, and loneliness—which appear in many different works.**

○ Incorrect. The story is about Cornelia defending the food she and her family are going to eat for Christmas, not about cooking.

● **Correct. Cornelia fights for the turkey and the rusks because she paid six dollars for the turkey and worked hard on the rusks. Her story teaches that protecting what a person has struggled to gain is a part of life.**

○ Incorrect. It is true that the turkey is difficult to obtain, but this is a detail of the story. A theme is a bigger idea about life that readers learn from the story. Knowing that the turkey was hard to get shows readers why Cornelia fights to keep it.

○ Incorrect. While generosity is often a virtue, in this story, Cornelia can only afford to be generous to her family. She does not show generosity to the soldiers; she fights to protect what is hers.

2. **Standard 7.3.2 Identify events that advance the plot and determine how each event explains past or present action or foreshadows (provides clues to) future action.**

○ Incorrect. Cornelia does feel bad that the wood her sons chopped is being stolen by the soldiers, but this is not what causes her to react with heroism.

○ Incorrect. Cornelia does not see the officer until after she stops the man from stealing the rusks. The officer does not inspire her to be bold.

○ Incorrect. Mary, not a soldier, points out that the rusks are being stolen. Cornelia herself decides to take action.

● **Correct. Cornelia had worked so long and carefully on the rusks that she hurt her wrists, and it was the first time she had ever made them. As a result, she was proud of the rusks and wanted to make sure that she and her family, not the soldiers, ate them.**

3. **Standard 7.2.4 Identify and trace the development of an author's argument, point of view, or perspective in text.**

Sample answer:
1) In "A Glimpse of War," Cornelia explains that good food like the turkey was expensive and rare. Both passages explain that hungry soldiers often took food from families. Since food was scarce, women had to hide it or fight for it.
2) In "Life at Home During the Civil War," the author explains that during the war, there was almost no new cloth. Women had to protect whatever old clothes or cloth they had in order to dress their families.

Answers will vary. Use the rubric on page 44 to score students' responses.

4. **Standard 7.1.3 Clarify word meanings through the use of definition, example, restatement, or through the use of contrast stated in the text.**

● **Correct. *Restore* is the root of *restoration*. To restore means "to give back" or "to return." When Cornelia demands the *restoration* of her property, she is telling the soldier to give it back.**

○ Incorrect. *Beautification* is the process of making something beautiful. Cornelia wants her turkey back; she does not need to have something made beautiful.

○ Incorrect. An exchange is made when someone trades an item for another item. Cornelia is not making an exchange; she wants the soldier to give back the turkey without having to trade something for it.

○ Incorrect. To capture something means to catch it. Cornelia wants her turkey back; she does not want something caught.

5. **Standard 7.3.3 Analyze characterization as shown through a character's thoughts, words, speech patterns, and actions; the narrator's description; and the thoughts, words, and actions of other characters.**

Sample answer:

What the soldiers steal	Why Cornelia cares
the turkey	because it cost her six dollars
the wood	because her sons had worked hard to cut it
the rusks	because they were the first she had ever made and she worked on them until her wrists hurt

Answers will vary. Use the rubric on page 44 to score students' responses.

Answers and Explanations for Instruction

6. **Standard 7.2.4 Identify and trace the development of an author's argument, point of view, or perspective in text.**

   ○ Incorrect. The passage explains that both soldiers and civilians had to be creative about finding food.

   ○ Incorrect. Soldiers stole horses from women, and some may have returned them in time; however, the passage does not state this.

   ○ Incorrect. According to the passage, neither soldiers nor civilians had coffee, sugar, or new clothes during the war.

   ● **Correct. The passage states that there was no sugar during the war, so both soldiers and civilians had to go without it.**

7. **Standard 7.2.6 Assess the adequacy, accuracy, and appropriateness of the author's evidence to support claims and assertions, noting instances of bias and stereotyping.**

   ● **Correct. The sentence states the women had to find the food; they had to come up with new ways to provide food for their families when it became too expensive to buy items such as flour.**

   ○ Incorrect. The sentence is about all Americans: men, women, and children. It is not specific evidence that women had to provide food for their families.

   ○ Incorrect. The sentence explains how people stored meat before refrigerators were invented. By itself, the sentence does not specifically tell how women provided for their families during the war.

   ○ Incorrect. The sentence is an example of how all Americans—women, men, and children—made do without tooth-brushes during the war. The sentence is not specific evidence about how women provided for their families.

8. **Standard 7.2.1 Understand and analyze the differences in structure and purpose between various categories of informational materials (such as textbooks, newspapers, and instructional or technical manuals).**

   Standard 7.2.4 Identify and trace the development of an author's argument, point of view, or perspective in text.

   ○ Incorrect. Knowing what kind of clothes soldiers wore in the Civil War does not help explain the events in the story. "A Glimpse of War" is about the scarcity of food during the war.

   ● **Correct. Understanding how little food there was during the war explains why Cornelia fought for the turkey and the rusks. It also explains why Cornelia wanted a Christmas turkey and sent a man miles away to get the turkey; it was to be a rare treat.**

   ○ Incorrect. Neither passage mentions what people fed their livestock during the war.

   ○ Incorrect. Cornelia is in the story, not in "Life at Home During the Civil War." She herself explains why she and the officer start laughing in "A Glimpse of War."

from The Raven (pages 88–93)

9. **Standard 7.2.4 Identify and trace the development of an author's argument, point of view, or perspective in text.**

   ○ Incorrect. In this line, the speaker remembers something; he does not reveal a feeling about what he remembers.
   ○ Incorrect. This line simply describes the silence. No emotions are described.
   ○ Incorrect. The speaker tells about his books, not his emotions.
   ● **Correct. The words *thrilled* and *terrors* reveal that the speaker feels fear and excitement.**

10. **Standard 7.3.4 Identify and analyze themes—such as bravery, loyalty, friendship, and loneliness—which appear in many different works.**

    Sample answer: Sorrow about a departed love is a main theme in the poem. Not only does the speaker whisper his lost love's name at the end of the poem because he wishes it were she tapping at the door, but he also says, "Eagerly I wished the morrow;—vainly I had sought to borrow/From my books surcease of sorrow—sorrow for the Lost Lenore."

    Answers will vary. Use the rubric on page 44 to score students' responses.

11. **Standard 7.3.2 Identify events that advance the plot and determine how each event explains past or present action or foreshadows (provides clues to) future action.**

    ○ Incorrect. These lines come after the speaker has heard the tapping for the first time; he has stopped reading and is imagining what could have made the tapping sound.
    ○ Incorrect. The emotions mentioned in these lines are fear and excitement. Lenore is not mentioned, nor is the speaker's sorrow.
    ● **Correct. These lines explain that when the speaker hears the tapping, he becomes afraid and imagines who or what could be at the door. Because he becomes so worried, he has to tell himself to calm down before opening the door.**
    ○ Incorrect. In the first part of the poem, the speaker is alone, reading calmly. His fear comes from the unexpected tapping.

12. **Standard 7.3.3 Analyze characterization as shown through a character's thoughts, words, speech patterns, and actions; the narrator's description; and the thoughts, words, and actions of other characters.**

    Sample answer:
    1) The speaker tries to ignore the tapping by saying that it is nothing, even after it starts to scare him.
    2) The speaker opens the door after hearing the tapping because he wants to see who it is, wishing it to be Lenore.

    Answers will vary. Use the rubric on page 44 to score students' responses.

Answers and Explanations for Instruction

13. **Standards 7.3 Reading: Reading Literary Response and Analysis; 7.5 Writing: Writing Applications; 7.6 Writing: Written English Language Conventions**

Sample answer:

The mood of this poem is serious and sad. The speaker misses a woman named Lenore very much—so much that everything he does and everything that happens to him reflects the sorrow he feels about losing Lenore.

For example, in the first three stanzas, the speaker describes the eerie or gloomy setting. He tells readers that it is a winter night with the phrases "midnight dreary" and "bleak December." He describes his fire by saying that each ember was "dying" and cast "its ghost" on the floor. When his curtains rustle, he says the sound is "sad, uncertain." All of these words make the poem's mood dark.

Also, the speaker reveals that Lenore is the motivation behind his actions in two key parts of the poem. First, he reads books to try to stop thinking about and missing Lenore. He calls her a "rare and radiant maiden" and says that angels named her. Second, he whispers her name at the end of the poem when he opens the door. He does this because he wishes she were there. Basing the poem on Lenore, whom he has lost, makes the mood sorrowful and intense.

Finally, the speaker ends each stanza with a line that ends with either "nothing more" or "ever more." These words emphasize his loss. This sad meaning makes the lines haunting.

The gloomy setting, the memories of Lenore, and the repetition that she is gone make the mood of this poem serious, sad, and eerie and make the reader doubt, fear, and dream just as the speaker does.

Answers will vary. Use the rubrics on pages 41–43 to score students' responses.

Scoring Rubrics

Scoring your students' responses to the Test 3 writing activity and Test 4 short-response and extended-response questions involves the use of four rubrics that rate students' mastery of the specific reading, writing, and language skills standards.

Use the following rubrics to determine correct responses to writing activity, short-response, and extended-response questions:

Modeled Instruction

Writing Applications Rubric:	pages 24–30 (Test 3)
Language Conventions Rubric:	pages 24–30 (Test 3), pages 41–43 (question 13)
Extended-Response Writing Applications Rubric:	pages 41–43 (question 13)
Short-Response Rubric:	page 35 (question 3), page 36 (question 5), page 39 (question 10), page 40 (question 12)

Practice Test

Writing Applications Rubric:	pages 73–79 (Test 3)
Language Conventions Rubric:	pages 73–79 (Test 3), pages 91–93 (question 13)
Extended-Response Writing Applications Rubric:	pages 91–93 (question 13)
Short-Response Rubric:	page 84 (question 3), page 85 (question 5), page 89 (question 10), page 90 (question 12)

Writing Applications Overview
Grades 6–12

Overview of the Writing Applications Rubric

The Writing Applications Rubric summarizes the requirements for each of the six score levels. Read across the rows to determine a specific score point's criteria.

Score Level	Ideas and Content	Organization
6	• Accomplishes task fully • Thorough, relevant, and complete ideas are included	• Logically organizes ideas
5	• Accomplishes task fully • Many relevant ideas are included	• Logically organizes ideas
4	• Accomplishes task • Relevant ideas are included	• Logically organizes ideas
3	• Accomplishes task minimally • Some relevant ideas are included	• Shows an attempt to logically organize ideas
2	• Accomplishes task partially • Few relevant ideas are included	• Shows a minimal attempt to logically organize ideas
1	• Does not accomplish task • Very few relevant ideas are included	• Illogically organizes ideas

Score Level	Style	Voice
6	• Demonstrates exceptional word usage and writing technique	• Language and tone are effectively adjusted to task and reader
5	• Demonstrates very good word usage and writing technique	• Language and tone are effectively adjusted to task and reader
4	• Demonstrates good word usage and writing technique	• An attempt to adjust language and tone to task and reader is shown
3	• Demonstrates ordinary word usage and average writing technique	• An attempt to adjust language and tone to task and reader is shown
2	• Demonstrates minimal word usage and writing technique	• Language and tone are inappropriate to task and reader
1	• Demonstrates less than minimal word usage and writing technique	• Language and tone are inappropriate to task and reader

Writing Applications Rubric

Grades 6-12

SCORE POINT 6
Ideas and Content

The writing sample fully accomplishes the task by focusing on the topic and presenting a unified theme or main idea with no tangents. It includes thorough, relevant, and complete ideas by fully exploring facets of the topic and including in-depth information and developed supporting details.

Organization

The writing sample's ideas are logically organized and presented meaningfully as a cohesive whole. It has a beginning, middle and end and progresses in a way that enhances meaning. Between ideas, sentences, and paragraphs, smooth transitions enhance the meaning of the text.

Style

The writing sample has exceptional word usage shown through the controlled use of challenging vocabulary words. The vocabulary is used to make precise, detailed explanations, rich descriptions, and clear, vivid actions. Exceptional writing techniques are shown through fluent writing. Varied sentence patterns, complex sentences too, are included. The writer's techniques like imagery/dialogue or humor/suspense are demonstrated.

Voice

The writing sample has language and tone effectively adjusted to task and reader. The voice exhibits the appropriate register and reflects a strong sense of audience. An original perspective is evident.

Language Conventions Rubric

Grades 6–12

Score 4	**A good command of language skills is shown in the writing sample**
	A Score Point 4 paper will have infrequent errors that are of the first-draft kind; overall communication is only slightly affected. The flow of communication will not be impaired. **Words have very few or no** • capitalization errors • spelling errors **Sentences have very few or no** • punctuation errors • grammar or word usage errors **Writing has very few or no** • paragraphing errors • run-on sentences or sentence fragments
Score 3	**A adequate command of language skills is shown in the writing sample**
	A Score Point 3 paper will have occasional errors, but these errors will not seriously impair the writer's meaning or flow of communication. **Words have occasional** • capitalization errors • spelling errors **Sentences have occasional** • punctuation errors • grammar or word usage errors **Writing has occasional** • paragraphing errors • run-on sentences or sentence fragments
Score 2	**A minimal command of language skills is shown in the writing sample**
	A Score Point 2 paper will have frequent errors that force the reader to stop and reread sections of the text. Communication will be impaired, but if the reader tries, he or she will be able to understand the writer's message. **Words have frequent** • capitalization errors • spelling errors **Sentences have frequent** • punctuation errors • grammar or word usage errors **Writing has frequent** • paragraphing errors or no paragraphing at all • run-on sentences or sentence fragments
Score 1	**A less than minimal command of language skills is shown in the writing sample**
	A Score Point 1 paper will have numerous errors that of a wide variety that prevent the reader from understanding the writer's message. **Words have many** • capitalization errors • spelling errors **Sentences have many** • punctuation errors • grammar or word usage errors **Writing has many** • paragraphing errors • run-on sentences or sentence fragments

Extended-Response Writing Applications Overview

Grades 6–12

Score 4	What the writing sample does
	• accomplishes the task fully
	• includes many relevant ideas
	• logically organizes ideas
	• shows very good word usage
	• exhibits very good writing technique
	• effectively adjusts language and tone for reader and task

Score 3	What the writing sample does
	• accomplishes the task
	• includes relevant ideas
	• logically organizes ideas
	• shows good word usage
	• exhibits good writing technique
	• attempts to adjust language and tone for reader and task

Score 2	What the writing sample does
	• accomplishes the task minimally
	• includes some relevant ideas
	• attempts to logically organize ideas
	• shows ordinary word usage
	• exhibits adequate writing technique
	• attempts to adjust language and tone for reader and task

Score 1	What the writing sample does
	• accomplishes the task partially or not at all
	• includes few relevant ideas
	• minimally attempts to logically organize ideas
	• shows minimal word usage
	• exhibits minimal or less than minimal writing technique
	• has inappropriate language and tone for reader and task

Extended-Response Writing Applications Rubric

Grades 6–12

SCORE POINT 4
Ideas and Content

The writing sample fully accomplishes the task by focusing on the topic and presenting a unified theme or main idea with no tangents. It gives plenty of information and develops more than adequate supporting details in order to explore different facets of the topic.

Organization

The writing sample's ideas are logically organized and presented meaningfully as a cohesive whole. It has a beginning, middle and end and progresses in a way that enhances meaning. Between ideas, sentences, and paragraphs, smooth transitions enhance the meaning of the text.

Style

The writing sample has very good word usage shown through the controlled use of vocabulary words. The vocabulary is used to make precise, detailed explanations, rich descriptions, and clear, vivid actions. Very good writing techniques are shown through fluent writing. Varied sentence patterns, complex sentences too, are included. The writer's techniques like imagery/dialogue or humor/suspense are demonstrated.

Voice

The writing sample has language and tone effectively adjusted to task and reader. The voice exhibits the appropriate register and reflects a sense of audience. An original perspective is evident.

Short-Response Rubric

The Short-Response Rubric is used to score the short-answer items that ask students for two pieces of information from a passage. If a student provides an answer that is not included in the list of sample exemplars, but the text supports the response, then the student should be given credit for the answer.

Short-Response Rubric	
Score 2	
	• Answer includes two exemplars from the passage
Score 1	
	• Answer includes one exemplar from the passage
Score 0	
	• Other

Teacher Notes

Teacher Notes